This Gratitude Journal Belongs To:

_____

_____

My Star Rating For Today

Today's Top 3 Best Moments

1.

2.

3.

Today I Am Grateful For...

The Most Awesome Thing That Happened Today Was...

My Thoughts...

My Doodles....

My Star Rating For Today

Today's Top 3 Best Moments

1.

2.

3.

Today I Am Grateful For...

The Most Awesome Thing That Happened Today Was...

My Thoughts...

My Doodles...

My Star Rating For Today

Today's Top 3 Best Moments

1.

2.

3.

Today I Am Grateful For...

The Most Awesome Thing
That Happened Today Was...

My Thoughts...

My Doodles....

My Star Rating For Today

Today's Top 3 Best Moments

1.

2.

3.

Today I Am Grateful For...

The Most Awesome Thing That Happened Today Was...

My Thoughts...

My Doodles....

My Star Rating For Today

Today's Top 3 Best Moments

1.

2.

3.

Today I Am Grateful For...

The Most Awesome Thing That Happened Today Was...

My Thoughts...

My Doodles...

My Star Rating For Today

Today's Top 3 Best Moments

1.

2.

3.

Today I Am Grateful For...

The Most Awesome Thing
That Happened Today Was...

My Thoughts...

My Doodles...

My Star Rating For Today

Today's Top 3 Best Moments

1.

2.

3.

Today I Am Grateful For...

The Most Awesome Thing
That Happened Today Was...

My Thoughts...

My Doodles....

My Star Rating For Today

Today's Top 3 Best Moments

1.

2.

3.

Today I Am Grateful For...

The Most Awesome Thing That Happened Today Was...

My Thoughts...

My Doodles....

My Star Rating For Today

Today's Top 3 Best Moments

1.

2.

3.

Today I Am Grateful For...

The Most Awesome Thing That Happened Today Was...

My Thoughts...

My Doodles....

My Star Rating For Today

Today's Top 3 Best Moments

1.

2.

3.

Today I Am Grateful For...

The Most Awesome Thing That Happened Today Was...

My Thoughts...

My Doodles...

My Star Rating For Today

Today's Top 3 Best Moments

1.

2.

3.

Today I Am Grateful For...

The Most Awesome Thing That Happened Today Was...

My Thoughts...

My Doodles....

My Star Rating For Today

Today's Top 3 Best Moments

1.

2.

3.

Today I Am Grateful For...

The Most Awesome Thing That Happened Today Was...

My Thoughts...

My Doodles....

My Star Rating For Today

Today's Top 3 Best Moments

1.

2.

3.

Today I Am Grateful For...

The Most Awesome Thing
That Happened Today Was...

My Thoughts....

My Doodles....

My Star Rating For Today

Today's Top 3 Best Moments

1.

2.

3.

Today I Am Grateful For...

The Most Awesome Thing That Happened Today Was...

My Thoughts....

My Doodles....

My Star Rating For Today

Today's Top 3 Best Moments

1.

2.

3.

Today I Am Grateful For...

The Most Awesome Thing
That Happened Today Was...

My Thoughts...

My Doodles....

My Star Rating For Today

Today's Top 3 Best Moments

1.

2.

3.

Today I Am Grateful For...

The Most Awesome Thing That Happened Today Was...

My Thoughts...

My Doodles....

My Star Rating For Today

Today's Top 3 Best Moments

1.

2.

3.

Today I Am Grateful For...

The Most Awesome Thing That Happened Today Was...

My Thoughts....

My Doodles....

My Star Rating For Today

Today's Top 3 Best Moments

1.

2.

3.

Today I Am Grateful For...

The Most Awesome Thing That Happened Today Was...

My Thoughts...

My Doodles...

My Star Rating For Today

Today's Top 3 Best Moments

1.

2.

3.

Today I Am Grateful For...

The Most Awesome Thing That Happened Today Was...

My Thoughts...

My Doodles...

My Star Rating For Today

Today's Top 3 Best Moments

1.

2.

3.

Today I Am Grateful For...

The Most Awesome Thing That Happened Today Was...

My Thoughts...

My Doodles....

My Star Rating For Today

Today's Top 3 Best Moments

1.

2.

3.

Today I Am Grateful For...

The Most Awesome Thing That Happened Today Was...

My Thoughts...

My Doodles...

My Star Rating For Today

Today's Top 3 Best Moments
1.
2.
3.

Today I Am Grateful For...

The Most Awesome Thing
That Happened Today Was...

My Thoughts...

My Doodles....

My Star Rating For Today

Today's Top 3 Best Moments

1.

2.

3.

Today I Am Grateful For...

The Most Awesome Thing That Happened Today Was...

My Thoughts...

My Doodles....

My Star Rating For Today

Today's Top 3 Best Moments

1.

2.

3.

Today I Am Grateful For...

The Most Awesome Thing
That Happened Today Was...

My Thoughts...

My Doodles....

My Star Rating For Today

Today's Top 3 Best Moments

1.

2.

3.

Today I Am Grateful For...

The Most Awesome Thing That Happened Today Was...

My Thoughts...

My Doodles....

My Star Rating For Today

Today's Top 3 Best Moments

1.

2.

3.

Today I Am Grateful For...

The Most Awesome Thing That Happened Today Was...

My Thoughts...

My Doodles....

My Star Rating For Today

Today's Top 3 Best Moments

1.

2.

3.

Today I Am Grateful For...

The Most Awesome Thing That Happened Today Was...

My Thoughts...

My Doodles....

My Star Rating For Today

Today's Top 3 Best Moments

1.

2.

3.

Today I Am Grateful For...

The Most Awesome Thing That Happened Today Was...

My Thoughts...

My Doodles...

My Star Rating For Today

Today's Top 3 Best Moments

1.

2.

3.

Today I Am Grateful For...

The Most Awesome Thing That Happened Today Was...

My Thoughts...

My Doodles...

My Star Rating For Today

Today's Top 3 Best Moments

1.

2.

3.

Today I Am Grateful For...

The Most Awesome Thing That Happened Today Was...

My Thoughts...

My Doodles....

CPSIA information can be obtained
at www.ICGtesting.com
Printed in the USA
LVOW04s0355271117
557668LV00026BA/1693/P

9 781976 413643